Character Education

Patriotism

by Lucia Raatma

Consultant:
Madonna Murphy, Ph.D.
Associate Professor of Education
University of St. Francis, Joliet, Illinois
Author, *Character Education in America's
Blue Ribbon Schools*

Bridgestone Books
an imprint of Capstone Press
Mankato, Minnesota

Bridgestone Books are published by Capstone Press
151 Good Counsel Drive, P.O. Box 669, Mankato, Minnesota 56002
http://www.capstone-press.com

Library of Congress Cataloging-in-Publication Data
Raatma, Lucia.
    Patriotism/by Lucia Raatma.
    p. cm.— (Character education)
    Includes bibliographical references and index.
    Summary: Explains the virtue of patriotism, or being proud of your country,
and describes ways to show patriotism at home, at school, and in the community.
    ISBN 0-7368-0509-5
    1. Patriotism—Juvenile literature. [1. Patriotism.] I. Title. II Series.
JC329 .R33 2000
320.54'0973—dc21   99-048335

Editorial Credits

Sarah Schuette, editor; Steve Christensen, cover designer; Kimberly Danger,
    photo researcher

Photo Credits

David F. Clobes, 6
Dennis Hallinan/FPG International LLC, 16; FPG International LLC, 18
Frances M. Roberts, 20
International Stock, 12
Matt Swinden, 10
Richard B. Levine, cover
The Picture Cube/Aneal Vohra, 4
Unicorn Stock Photos/Jean Higgins, 8; Macdonald Photos, 14

1 2 3 4 5 6 05 04 03 02 01 00

Table of Contents

Patriotism

Patriotism means being proud of and loyal to your country. Patriotic people work to make their country a better place to live. They vote in elections. They respect their country's symbols. You are patriotic when you salute your country's flag.

loyal
faithful to your country

The Congress
of the
United States

by David Heath

Being Patriotic

People of all ages can help improve their country. You can be patriotic by learning how the U.S. government works. Learn how to make changes in government. Write a letter to your senators. Ask them to change laws to help improve the country.

senator

a person who represents a state in U.S. Congress; Congress makes the country's laws.

Patriotism with Your Family

Your family can be patriotic by celebrating national holidays together. You and your family can attend a parade together on Independence Day. You can visit a veteran's grave on Memorial Day.

veteran

someone who has served in the armed forces

Patriotism with Your Friends

The U.S. government is a democracy. A democracy is a government run by the people. Practice democracy with your friends. You may not all agree what to do one afternoon. Listen to everyone's ideas. Take a vote. Then follow the ideas of the majority.

majority

more than half of
a group of people

11

Patriotism in Sports

You can show pride for your country during the Olympic Games. The Olympic Games are sports contests between athletes from many countries around the world. Cheer for your country's athletes and teams.

athlete
a person trained
in a sport or game

Patriotism at School

You can be patriotic at school. Say the Pledge of Allegiance with your class. Learn about American history. Many people worked and fought to protect the United States. Read about national heroes. Understand how their work affects your life.

Pledge of Allegiance
a promise to be loyal
to the United States

Patriotism in Your Community

People show patriotism in many ways. Some people fly the U.S. flag in front of their homes. You also can show your patriotism at sporting events. Stand and sing the national anthem when it is played before the game.

national anthem

a song that represents a country; "The Star-Spangled Banner" is the national anthem of the United States.

"One of the highest duties of a citizen is...obedience to the laws of the nation."
—Thomas Jefferson

Patriotic Thomas Jefferson

Thomas Jefferson served as U.S. president from 1801 to 1809. Thomas also helped write the Declaration of Independence. He worked hard so all people in the U.S. would have freedom. Thomas showed patriotism by working to improve the country.

Declaration of Independence

a document that made the U.S. free from Britain in 1776

Patriotism and You

Citizens of the United States have many rights. They are free to practice their own religion. Citizens are free to share their ideas. Understanding your rights can help you be patriotic. Patriotic people make the United States safer and stronger.

citizen
a member of a particular country who has the right to live there

Hands On: Hold an Election

Voting in elections is one way adult citizens voice their ideas. Ask your teacher to help you hold a classroom election.

What You Need
A piece of paper for each classmate
A large box with a hole in the top
Pencils or pens

What You Do
1. Hold a meeting with your class. Discuss changes you can make in your school or class.
2. Hold an election when your class has chosen one good idea.
3. Write the idea on the board. Write the idea in the form of a question. For example, "Should the class plan a holiday party?"
4. Give each student a piece of paper. The paper is the ballot.
5. Have each person write "yes" or "no" on the ballot.
6. Have each person fold the paper and put it into the box.
7. Ask your teacher to count the votes.
8. If your class votes to approve the idea, discuss it with your teacher. Plan how to make the idea work.

Your teacher may not agree with your class' idea. But you can see how elections work. Adult citizens vote in elections to make changes in a country's government.

Words to Know

citizen (SIT-i-zuhn)—a member of a particular country who has the right to live there

democracy (di-MOK-ruh-see)—a government in which people choose their leaders by voting

document (DOK-yoo-muhnt)—a piece of paper containing important information

loyal (LOI-uhl)—faithful to your country

majority (muh-JOR-uh-tee)—more than half of a group of people

symbol (SIM-buhl)—an object that represents something else; a flag is a symbol of a country.

veteran (VET-ur-uhn)—someone who has served in the armed forces

Read More

Pingry, Patricia. *The Story of America's Birthday.* Nashville, Tenn.: Candy Cane Press, 1999.
Usel, T. M. *Thomas Jefferson.* Photo-Illustrated Biographies. Mankato, Minn.: Bridgestone Books, 1996.

Internet Sites

Kids Voting USA—Students Only
http://www.kidsvotingusa.org/students.html
Symbols and Celebrations—Americana FAQs
http://www.usia.gov/usa/usa.htm/facts/symbols.htm
USA Government
http://pittsford.monroe.edu/schools/jefferson/
   government/govhome.html

Index